D1279925

Penn Hills Library
0 Aster Street
sburgh, PA 15235

The Origins of Evening

Penn Hills Library
240 Aster Street
Pittsburgh, PA 15235

THE NATIONAL POETRY SERIES

*The National Poetry Series was established in 1978 to
ensure the publication of five poetry collections annually through
participating publishers. Publication is funded by James A.
Michener, The Copernicus Society of America, Edward J. Piszek,
The Lannan Foundation, and the Tiny Tiger Foundation.*

1997 Winners

Sandra Alcosser of Montana, *Except by Nature*
Chosen by Eamon Grennan, to be published by Graywolf Press

Martine Bellen of New York City,
Tales of Murasaki and Other Poems
Chosen by Rosmarie Waldrop, to be published by
Sun & Moon Press

Robert Gibb of Pittsburgh, *The Origins of Evening*
Chosen by Eavan Boland, to be published by W. W. Norton

Lisa Lewis of Oklahoma, *Silent Treatment*
Chosen by Stanley Plumly, to be published by Penguin Books

Heather Ramsdell of Brooklyn, *Lost Wax*
Chosen by James Tate, to be published by
University of Illinois Press

ALSO BY ROBERT GIBB

ENTERED APR 1999

The Origins of Evening

POEMS

811.54
GIB

Winner of the 1997 National Poetry Series

Robert Gibb

W. W. NORTON & COMPANY

NEW YORK • LONDON

PENN HILLS LIBRARY

Copyright © 1998 by Robert Gibb

All rights reserved
Printed in the United States of America
First Edition

For information about permission to reproduce selections from this book,
write to Permissions, W. W. Norton & Company, Inc., 500 Fifth Avenue,
New York, NY 10110.

The text of this book is composed in Bodoni Book
with the display set in Industria Solid Roman
Composition on desktop by Gina Webster
Manufacturing by The Courier Companies, Inc.
Bood design by BTD/Beth Tondreau

LIBRARY OF CONGRESS CATALOGING-IN-PUBLICATION DATA
Gibb, Robert.
The origins of evening : poems / Robert Gibb.
p.   cm.
ISBN 0-393-04644-3
I. Title
PS3557.I139065   1998
811'.54—dc21   97–39454
                                CIP

W. W. Norton & Company, Inc., 500 Fifth Avenue, New York, N.Y. 10110
http://www.wwnorton.com

W. W. Norton & Company, Ltd., 10 Coptic Street, London WC1A 1PU

1 2 3 4 5 6 7 8 9 0

ACKNOWLEDGMENTS

*Grateful acknowledgment is made to the following publications in which
these poems previously appeared:*
Antaeus: "In the Carnegie Museum"
Apalachee Quarterly: "The Closet"
Carolina Quarterly: "Entering the Oven"
Cincinnati Poetry Review: "Ohio"
Creeping Bent: "From the Book of Dreams"
Cutbank: "The Adorations"
Field: "Japanese"
Hampden-Sydney Review: "How Trees Are Known and Named"
Hiram Poetry Review: "Memory: A Poem for a Möbius Strip"
The Illinois Review: "Swimming Lessons"
Ironwood: "Letter to a Friend's Wife"
The Kenyon Review: "Moths"
The Laurel Review: "Tomatoes"
The Missouri Review: "Fathers and Sons," "Seeing Pittsburgh," "Home,"
        "First Day," and "Aubade"
New England Review: "Flashbulbs"
New Letters: "Song for My Father"
Painted Bride Quarterly: "Letter to Russell Barron"
Poetry: "The Race" and "Lines in a Slow Thaw"
Poetry Northwest: "On First Viewing *The Deer Hunter*: Boyd Theater,
        Bethlehem, 1978" (under the title "Home Movies")
Porch: "The Origins of Evening" and "Last Things"
Prairie Schooner: "Sitting in the Dark"
The Quarterly: "Fire Poem," "The Knife," and "Since History Is a
        Marriage of Geography and Race"
Quarterly West: "Rogation Sunday"

The Southern Review: "St. Paul's Union Church and Cemetery,
　　　Seiberlingsville, Pennsylvania" and "The Shape of the Goddess in
　　　Homestead Park"
Sou'wester: "The Holy Days" and "Granville Beitel"
The Widener Review: "Salt"
Willow Springs: "Among the Successions"
Wind: "Sixteenth Avenue"

"Letter to Russell Barron" appeared in *Sweet Nothings: An Anthology of
Rock and Roll in American Poetry*, edited by Jim Elledge (Indiana
University Press, 1994).

"Flash Bulbs" was included in the 1995/1996 *Anthology of Magazine
Verse & Yearbook of American Poetry*.

"The Race" is included in FATHERS: *A Collection of Poems*, edited by
David and Judy Ray, St. Martin's Press, 1997.

Acknowledgment, and thanks, is also due The Pennsylvania Council on
the Arts for a grant during a crucial period in the writing of this book.

Contents

In memory of my mother and father

Not the thin, shed, bodies of light
Blown and chambered as honeycombs—

Here the whole skins of snakes
Coil about the limbs of trees

Or the one long bough of their bodies,
In cases slim as scabbards

Where they lie unsheathed like fangs,
Or displays in which they seethe

Almost audibly out onto the air
Where something still is hanging,

Cold-blooded and incumbent as loss.
My stepmother brought me here once

To watch the tranced dance of Hopis
Blend their bodies into snakes.

Each enraptured length heavy with scales,
Each head pressed out like a thumb,

And the socket and scald of heaven
Only a wrong move off. Upstairs,

In their staged pueblos, mannequins
Made pots and blankets, cradled

Prayer sticks. The gown of a bending
Woman hung down from breasts

Which were the roundness of the world
Transfigured in my eager sight.

The corded sinews blood-jammed
And pulsing, sunlight falling

Through the leaves in their veins . . .

There must be some way to enter
The world and keep on moving into it,

Leaving the old life, rung by rattles,
Lying there in the dark.

Moths

I like the leaf ones best,
For whom the ends of transformation
Are resemblance
To another life entirely—
The wings almost deciduous,
Antennae fusty as fronds.
As the one I saw last night
Fastened upon the screen
Seemed to have been blown there
By the wind, another scrap
Stuck fast from the hickories.
Even its patterns were patient
Arrangements of the dust:
Flocked, dry pigments
On which the night air fell.
It was still there in the morning,
Holding itself motionless
Into the world of forms.

In school we learned how molt
Follows molt into the magnitudes—
Successions of instars
Like Stations of the Cross.
How the moth is a mausoleum
Or cobwebbed vault.
That summer I broke my collarbone
The stiff cast held my shape
Even when they'd removed it,

Another unhasped casing
Left to its tree. Even then
       Change was a rending.
   Even the saints, we learned,
Had first to shed the chrysalis
       Which blocked their sight,
    Feeling themselves bleed outward
Into their wings
       Before lifting from the bark.

Fathers and Sons

Those days my father would collapse—
        Go down, stricken, on all fours
Like a beast of burden
        In a brute stupor of barbiturates—
We'd find him, massive with shadows
        On the floor, face down
Where the uncertain color of the carpet
        Trapped whatever light
He tried to stop breathing forever.
        After they'd strapped him upon
The gurney and wheeled him off
        Toward the gray world of the ward,
I still could see him, strewn in that pose
        Of one who has fallen from heaven,

All the way to Emsworth where I spent
        His recoveries at my aunt's.
While they steeped his days in Thorazine
        And numb, shuffling hours,
I had hedgerows and alleys, her awninged
        Porch. Those winters I watched
As chains of ice blocked the Ohio River
        Like another lock on the dam.
Summers, it flowed freely as sap
        From trees I'd flayed alive.
My cousin took me into woods
        And, holding my hand in her own,
Took me for a walk, one afternoon,
        Up the cindered drive of Bedlam.

The inmates, clamoring, almost human,
                    Pressed themselves against
The wire-embedded glass.
          The trees clamored later in my sleep.
I had never seen so much pain before,
                    Or held the way
Light shook me wholly into my senses,
          The inmates glowing above us
Like angels from their tiers.
                    The next time I saw my father,
He was beatific with insulin
          And rounds of electric current: cured,
Removed from the angels,
                    Restored to the haunts of God.

Seeing Pittsburgh

Is what it's called. What it is
Is a packet of photographs
      That unfold together, back to back,
In a pleat of twenty graphic views

    Of 1938. Black and white,
They are dyed the hard primary colors
      Raphael used in his painting
Of the Virgin, the *Madonna*

    del Gardellino, a composition
Remarkable for its triangles,
      The pale flame suffusing their peak
In the shape of a woman's face.

    Here the triangle lies upon its back
Between rivers pointing west,
      And is filled with buildings,
Bridges like buttresses holding it

    In place: a city in the confluence.
This is the point Washington
      Fell back from in 1755, where
My grandfather found in America

    The Glasgow he'd left behind—
The God whose eye was anthracite,
      Whose breath was the cloud of fire
Which hovered over Homestead.

In this picture you can see
The mills in which he died. Here
              Are the Fair Grounds at South Park,
The Race Track where I picture him

              At the turn of the century,
Like Cagney in *The Strawberry Blond.*
              This is the Leona Theater
Where every Saturday we lived

              In the earthly heaven of the movies,
The back rows where flesh took hold
              Of the breath in that building
Of peeling angels falling

              From the ceiling and light
Falling its incredible miles
              Per second onto the screen,
The sky above the mills a grainy mauve

              Feathering into ash above the rivers,
The slow flashings of their skins.
              This is what I mean, here
In this one, and here again.

              Here you'll have to imagine water
The way I did at night, rising
              Level by level up the hill,
A whole town loosed from its moorings,

Trolleys bobbing on their lines
To the carbarns and back again.
        These are the barges I watched haul
Flat tracts of iron ore, those rusted

    Acres, along the Monongahela.
This one glimmered into evening,
        Summers at its wharf, beneath
The *Water Music*'s magic notes.

    Every morning our windows opened
Onto this same handful of scenes.
        Here is Horseshoe Curve.
Here you can barely see the corner

    Of the Carnegie Museum. Back there
Is where I took my time, breathing
        The air as it settled like dusk
In the fall of a girl's soft hair.

    These are her wrists, the tongue
Of her hands. This is the dark
        I had to be home before. And then
Home in. And this is the dark of home.

    The Buhl Planetarium. The sullen
Massiveness of the Bloomfield Bridge.
        Rivers brown and thick as oil.
Air like dark bread . . .

Time must smell like this.
Time must fold back against itself,
        Vantage inside of vantage, creased
And enveloped, the corners wearing thin.

        Think of Einstein in his trolley.
Think of him moving at the speed of light
        And the people on the sidewalks
Going their glimpsed and quiet ways.

Fire Poem

This was before the wood
Behind our house was torn down
And sectioned into suburbs,
Before the trolleys stopped
Humming like hanging lamps.

I had yet to unfasten the pale
Fronts of blouses, or labor
All night in the deafening mills.
Slag heaps were still sunsets
On the far shores of Clairton

And railroads simply carried
Their ignitions past our home.
It would be years until ECT's
Began burning my father's brain,
And years more than that until

He was flashed all to ashes.
I had never even heard the word
Incineration before I helped
Unload the car. Before I stood
Swaying as the man slid back

The immense slab of concrete
And I saw beneath our streets
That all I had thought of as solid
Was empty instead, and enormous,
And a place of continuous flame.

Letter to a Friend's Wife

My answer is
A wine cup, full of the
Moon drowned in the River.
—Su Tung P'o

Some of us drink
To keep from catching on fire,
Others because the nerves
Juice down
To one wire, singing and clean
And burning with God's own
Electricity.
Some just because they are thirsty,
Or because the blue at evening
On the swallows' wings
Is almost too beautiful to bear.
My widowed father, who hid
One perfect, untouched bottle
In the rafters, was an alcoholic
Because he was afraid
Of becoming a drunk.
He did not know
That warm wine was better than water,
Or that, given his life,
It was decency he needed to fear,
And his second wife.
Any life where a man

Cannot go down on his knees,
Drunk or sober, in ecstasy
Is not worth the pain.
And who goes down sober?
Given the choice
Who would not rather die outward
Believing they were a light
No matter how much darkness
They drank?
Had you thought otherwise?
I think there are many ways to die,
And abstinence among them
Is one of the worst.
So you see
I have no comfort to send,
There being so many things in the world
That are indefensible
By which we make our way.

On First Viewing The Deer Hunter:
Boyd Theater, Bethlehem, 1978

That gray is just the way I remember,
Spilling out of night and the mills' dream
Of eternity as an endless turning
Of gears. The day climbs its cold ladders.
The waters of the Monongahela
Glint past houses and streets, the shale-toned
Light in which my face pulls back to the bone.
Here in the dark I watch the life I led
Go on without me: the Pittsburgh there
On the screen, and the further one beyond
Where my days were woods and sandlots, longings,
Fights in alleys after school. Where desire
Was that terrible glory for whatever bones
You managed to find against your own.

                    *

The mills were what held us, all those years,
The gears I thought of as time's. Summers
I dreamt of rivers riffling through the leaves.
Winters, I remember trees like stricken nerve-
Ends bolting all across the city,
Rimed with salt and the air that fell upon us
Covering everything. Snow lay pitted
And gray against the traffic. Roses
Were the color of thorns, of rivers and streets
Which circled back, it seemed, without end,

The halation lamps burning off their bleak
Unearthly vapors, the heavens above them
Above their banks and wandering like
The waters for the remainder of the night.

Memory: A Poem
for a Möbius Strip

I take them up
And turn them
In my hands—:

The rooms I could
Move through at night,
Even now, without

Brushing against
A thing. I could
Show you distances

I learned by heart
Between the front
Porch and where

The wisteria bloomed
Each summer
Back beneath the trees.

I could tally
The heart's beads
One by one,

And the dark
Would be the same
Long passage of water

Through the night,
The moon climbing
Its trellis,

The roses twisting
Up their thorns.
That tree struck by

Lightning 20 years
Ago would fork into
Blossom once more.

There are moments
In which it all
Comes flashing back.

They are like stones
In the garden
After it's rained,

Which have gleamed
Their dark way
To the surface.

I take them up
And turn them
In my hands—.

Japanese

Horned and iridescent
As metallic paint

They are, in themselves,
Beautiful jewels.

They refract the light
From their facets,

Their laminal backs,
Gold verging on verdigris

There on the beach-
Peas' flutter of flesh.

Only when you find them
In your garden,

Filigreeing the leaves,
Or groping blindly upon

Each other in those
Slow mineral ecstasies,

Do you remember the roses
Your stepmother mourned,

Dusting the blown
And tattered blossoms.

And whether in praise
Of perishing things

Or sorrow's love of them,
You move through the rows,

The two stones flat as
The palms of your hands,

Plagued by such beauty,
And clap.

St. Paul's Union Church and Cemetery, Seiberlingsville, Pennsylvania

Even their stones are frail,
Their names dissolving
In the slow caresses of weather,
As though once again they were giving up
Something of themselves.

So the dead are shelved.
Or, if you'd rather,
They float out upon the darkness
In the pale skiffs of their bones.
They empty and empty.

I'd envy their idleness,
If that's what it was,
Sunlight spilling onto marble
And lawn, the cast-gray irises
Sprouting from the fence.

It's been a long time since
I've sat among them,
Or thought about the stark hills
Of headstones flanking the road
That wound toward the river

Back home. Unlike this
Spare, unravished ground,
They were the great parishes
We came to, wild for the way moonlight
Lay gleaming upon our flesh.

Above us, the constellations
Lit up their acres, cold points of fire
              Connecting the heavens
        Into anatomy, and the bones
          In those dark meadows

          Buried beneath our clothes.
I'd like to come up here some evening
              With this woman that I know
          And rumple the folds
            Of her cool summer dress,

          Lifting myself among them
Until crickets were no longer singing
              Only outside our skins
          As we rubbed free, for the moment,
            Of all about us that was dead.

II

The Connection to the Dark

1. HOME

All those years, early or late,
It is evening and I am going home.
It is ham steak or cabbage,
And my father looks up from his plate,
And the woman who dresses us both
Cuts into the meal of leather and bone

And in a voice hard as her fingers
Says, "Your dinner's in the oven
Getting cold." Home is where
Such scenes seemed to linger,
Where you lost the first fears
Of dying or being orphaned.

There your father wept at meals,
The woman in her garden
Raged among the weeds, the roses whose sprays
Were overblown and blistered with weals.
The house was gray,
And the streets the color of rain

Falling from the First Book of Kings.
The color of the river
Being freighted past the mills
Where gray was made, where pouring

From the flues you watched it until
No matter where you were

Everywhere was home.

2. SIXTEENTH AVENUE

Prayers over, I am in bed.
The mystery of my sex and death
Has not yet begun

To keep me awake
Like the mystery of the dark,
Of where winds go,

Or why no one else hears the waters
Of the Monongahela
Rising nightly above its banks.

This is the house
In which my father was orphaned
Once by each parent,

And once by the priest
Who forgave my mother everything
So she might die

Here where winds die nightly
In the dry stairs and balustrades
Creaking like trees.

My door cracks open,
And my father empties the room
Of everything

Save the smell of his breath.
I can hear the dice in his joints
As he bends down toward me

To talk of sons, of my being the last
Unless like him I die
Once removed from what follows.

He wants to be continued,
Wants his name in nurseries
Again and again, wrapped

About the smallest of wrists
Like tags on bundles of cuttings.
Not until later, in a dream,

Does my mother come to tell me
Of that pale laughter
There in the heart of the wood.

3. THE RACE

This dream is green
And actual memory:
My father and I
In the neighbor's yard,

Having just stepped
Forth from the woods,
In summer, evening,
The light gone gauzy

About the shrubbery.
Perhaps it is joy
In the strangeness
Of our being together

Alone in such a place,
Or maybe it's only
The way the lawn slopes
Down its long expanse

Into our own backyard
That makes me dare him
To the race, first
One home the winner.

And am halfway there
And certain when he

Simply passes me by,
His trousers a thresh

Of fabric flowing
Smoothly on my right,
And then the amazing
Sight of him running

Steadily beyond me,
This father of chairs
And silences, halt
Figure of my youth.

How could I know then
My pursuit of him
Would never again come
Gladly to such an end?

4. HOW TREES ARE KNOWN AND NAMED

Often I am at a loss to know
More than the general constellations
Of branch, bole, and leaf.
    I can point to the obvious birches,
        The dusk-hued blue of the spruce.

The hedge that grew at my parents'
Was simply green: a tunnel
I could hide in, that hid
    The face of the house. Sycamores
        Were easy with their jigsaw bark,

And the locust in our backyard
With its thorns and bell-shaped
Blossoms. Any tree near your bed
Is known and named, any stillness
        Like sleep, any tree of heaven.

When lightning forked the locust
It was one tree lit with another,
Crown and root, clear to the ground.
    Summers filled with the green fire
        Of streetlights nestled in limbs,

The calm, enduring mysteries
Of the maple and the oak,

With the way our hands glowed
When pressed against the flashlight,
Veined and palmate as leaves.

5. FROM THE BOOK OF DREAMS

In my *Tempest* dream the winds
Whirl up out of the ends of my arms
Like game birds in open country,
Out of all proportion to myself.
Winds as vast as the constellations.
Overhead, stars have the color
Of hailstones or heaven in the kind
Of books I read when I was a boy.
The open fields are softly rolling,
The broomgrass plated as the sea.

It is like my dream of flight,
The one in which I balance myself
Out onto the air and rise in
A hovering delight, only there
My features are filled with evening
As it settles into the robes of earth.
In neither dream is the air anything
Other than a body abutting my own.
Like sleep. Like the soft curve
Of darkness on the face of the deep.

The pages of the dreambook are filled
With animals and gardens, bodies
Of water, their round light winking
Through the trees. When I was a boy

I believed in sleep as a passage,
A way from here to there, miraculous
As traveling through time. Nothing
I've dreamt since has changed that—
Not even the shadow who told me
That man is a disconsolate companion,

Or that carcass hanging before me,
Marbled with fat and jelled blue veins,
The lopped ribs flaring like wings.

6. TOMATOES

The patch sat at the end of our driveway,
    Stunted tomatoes tied to their stakes
        With rags, old nylons, a triage
    Next to where the car turned round.

And nothing else growing but weeds,
    Nothing else struggling up the knots
        Of light but the bruise-like blossoms
    Of her veins the morning I find

My stepmother crying she has nothing
    To keep her there among the rinsed
        Gray leaves, or in the meager house
    Beyond them where my father's waiting

On the line. She is leaving, she says,
    Because I haven't done my chores,
        Because our attic was never finished,
    The locust sheds too many twigs.

Because my father is human, after all,
    And Pittsburgh is a dark, filthy town.
        Ripping out fistfuls of weeds
    From that still damp ground,

She refuses to speak on the phone:
    "Tell your father if I decide to stay

It won't be on account of him."
Words which, even then, I know better

Than to repeat, though I carry them back
    With me, along with those tomatoes
        She's heaped into my arms, each one
Of them small and green and hard.

7. AMONG THE SUCCESSIONS

The connection to the dark
Occurs like this, in daylight,

Simply by emptying the barrow,
Wheeling it back into the yard,

And seeing my father emerging
Once more from the woods

With me riding before him
Above the dint and clattering wheel.

That was the summer he made
The rock garden for his wife,

Leaning those weekend muscles
Into shovels and freighted loads,

Sifting dirt through wire screens,
Fitting the chiseled stones.

All for a patch of caked soil
And ruin where nothing really grew.

But that wasn't until later.
Here I am watching him eye me

As a child, and understanding
How such idleness looks to men

Whose labors will come to naught
And who know it, and also know

That one load changes to another
Soon enough: ease to ache,

Dirt to delighted boy, to one
Stunned at finding himself

Among such successions, having
Come this late to the knowledge

That the loves of the father
Also are visited upon the son.

The Shape of the Goddess in Homestead Park

The first breast I even touched by accident,
Though I ached to lay such shining on my desire,
Was the left breast of Jimmy Markowitz's younger sister.

One half of the other part of the tussle
Beneath the backboard, she was only another
Heft and balance fighting for the ball.

I wasn't even looking at her when it happened.
And it happened long enough for me to understand
A more important roundness was now in my hand.

I wonder if she remembers that when I turned
I found her smiling at me with the kind of eyes
I wouldn't be ready for for years?

There was already something in her
Which was soft and warm, and dark like stables.
Her breasts were doves.

It's taken me all these years to reach back
To her and understand the darkness surrounding
Certain women is teeming and rich as topsoil.

Earthworms are singing through it,
And leaves breaking into loam, and an old sorrow,
Sweet as pye-weed, which rises from the dark.

Salt

Rivers and bridges, pitted brick,
      The dark wings of the mills . . .
I look up from my desk

Or off along the roadsides
      And what I see shimmers into street-
Lamps and shade trees, islands

For the trolleys, or those
      Blocks around Corbett's Drug Store
Where I wandered, first home

From grade school, then back across
      That earlier ground, prowling
Through alleys and vacant lots

As though drawn already by loss.
      Why else would the paving-stones
Bruise me still, or the glossy

Air-brushed months mounded to
      Nipple on the calendars in Park's
Luncheonette, its waitresses ruing

Their veins? Would these trees
      Keep blooming, cool and dark
As rainwater from the barrel we

Kept out back, if the past were
      Not insistent upon its witness,
Time upon how it enters the earth

Like water? Or the rain of traffic
      Upon the stones: glazed loaves,
Streets flashing through the lattices

Of the brain. Small wonder
      If again today it has seemed to me
That memory was a kind of hunger

Burning within the body like salt.

Lines in a Slow Thaw

Now this is more to my liking,
    This gentle run-off of water

From the fields, snow sintering
    Down to where the dandelion

Lies dreaming about its slender
    White root. I'd like to lose

Myself in such weather, watching
    Sparrows which are pecks of light

Flaring from their hedges.
    I'd like to be able to walk

Among the ruins of scrubweed
    And thistle and common dock

Without being reminded that snow
    Is melting on the cold shoulders

Of mills back home in the Mon
    River valley, and on houses

The color of dark, wet leaves.
    I'd rather not be reminded

Of any of what gets between me
    And my love for these mild

Freshets balming the earth.
　　I already know what waters

Seep on down from Homestead
　　And McKeesport into the heart

And that nothing I do is likely
　　To change them. I know this thaw

Is going to sidle into winter
　　For a long time still to come.

But that doesn't mean I'm going
　　To write down only the chronologies

Of ice, or behave as if rivers
　　Weren't pure economic theory.

I can't even watch for long
　　Before the gentle lave of water

Across the fields reminds me
　　Of my father's people in 1892—

Those photographs from the lockout,
　　Millworkers watching upriver

For scabs to come riding down
　　The first brown froth of flood.

The Holy Days

An old sun, gray north, and light
Falling past the windows like a dry

Perishable snow. The wind, you said,
Rises over Homestead

Like a terrible fish. Just blocks
From where these cold streets stop

The Monongahela spreads its scales,
Its dull flat back, beneath the mills.

Smoke and December 1968
Darken above the city.

At 4:00 P.M. the changing shifts
Pass in Snow's Tavern on Sixth

Avenue—Hungarians, Poles, and Serbs
Working at their endless thirsts,

The dialect coke and pig iron
Leave upon the tongue.

The nails of their hands are tempered,
Skin seared, eyes full of furnaces

And boilermakers, the sallow
Pallor of their flesh. Our shadows

Deepen in the mirror behind the bar.
The radio's hosannas and clatter

Fall upon us all: the passed over
And transient, the workers

Whose dreams are metal, blood,
The cindery breath of God,

Whose faith is the waters beyond them
Which tinder daily into flame.

Rogation Sunday

Some Sundays after church
My father and I would walk down
        The remaining rungs of hillside
    To where his office lay buried
Almost under the High Level Bridge.

Then, as if we had not descended
Enough, he'd unlock the doors
        And we'd step below street level,
    Down buffed marble stairs,
To the display-room floor. There

The appliances stood, still
And empty as tombs. Each one opened
        Upon the miraculous it offered.
    Each the temperature, I imagined,
Of the body stretched out cold.

Back beyond his plate-glass walls
My father sat, catching up with
        What was about to come at him
    Again, the very next morning,
Like the oncoming lane. Only then

Would I be permitted to sit behind
That desk, watching his white shirt
        Vanish on down the hallway
    Toward the storeroom and its files.
I'd fill up tablets with scribbles,

Grow bored and poke through
The drawers—fingering ink stamps
        And signets, the letter opener's
    One thin tine—or look out
To where the river ran, swollen

    With our sins. When he'd finished
We'd lock back up, then catch
        The trolley on home to papers
    And the remainder of a day
Whose routines I do not remember.

    There is nothing of Sunday drives
Or dinners. Only scraps
        Of sermon, like *light* and *stone*,
    And my father in that hallway,
His white shirt salt and bone.

The Knife

It is always in December, no matter when,
    This stillness cindering into gray,
        The flakes as light as ashes.

I stand on my porch, watching snow
    Fall upon the rolled grain of blacktop
        Until it starts to haze.

Soon it will be covered. At some point
    Everything we are or have meant to be
        Will be as endless and white.

Yet even here there are distances
    I stare across to where it's always
        Summer and all along Alberta Street

The maples float upward in lamplight.
    Whenever it is, Morgan and I are
        Halfway through our teens and dying

For the bird-shaped breasts of creatures
    Who used to be girls. Our aches
        Are simpler then, our dreams

Driving Chevies, moons on all four wheels,
    Up and down the streets of heaven
        In Homestead, Pennsylvania.

We have not yet stumbled into the ovens
        Of steel mill and marriage. Tonight
                It is his father who careens

Into the room, smiling and drunk,
        And holding against his mouth
                The blood-soaked towel and knife

He's been using to pry loose a tooth.
        Through that smear of grin
                He talks to us about the ways

To get at pain, about buckrubs
        And legs gnawed off in traps.
                His towel flowers with the shapes

Of his song, the maples lift into night
        Again this evening, snow falling
                Slantwise along their branches.

Everywhere I look it's cold, December,
        The year sliding further away.
                And yet it's still the knife,

Forged and honed and the way he holds it,
        That cuts, even now, until
                The sharp air tastes of metal.

First Day

Still astonished to be starting
      Work at twelve o'clock at night,
I passed through the dark streets
      By the river, that first Sunday
In another life, carrying my lunch-
      Box and steel-toed shoes toward
Those enormous ovens I'd be
      Laboring beneath till morning.
Left alone below the mill floor,
      I shoveled shale into the waters
Rushing beyond me like an opened
      Main, and could hear above me
The shear and clamor of metals,
      Crane whistles, ingots thundering
Along their beds to be rolled
      Through a series of presses.
I learned that day how time ran
      In the gears and drive trains
Of machinery, how time burned
      Inside furnaces in the great fires
Of creation and spread out evenly
      In sheets of steel. That night,
For the first time, I counted
      The hours coming on, one by one,
And passed through them without
      Sleep. Finally, that morning,
I watched the sun bloom in a sky
      Filled with mill smoke and

Sparrows rising from their baths
    Of dust, the blue fuse of ozone
From the wires above the trolleys.
    I learned how each new day
Was a promise light made to dust
    Before breaking, which the river
Took with it and emptied downstream.
    How the streets were a promise,
And the surge of current through
    The line—a song that the blood,
The humming wires, would take up
    Again with each new morning,
Just as though it were the first.

Ohio

I thought of it as all lawn, westering
And level, wide as the night sky.
I thought it was one bank, running
North along the river, one blunt line
On the map crimping its slow way south.
I thought it was more Pittsburgh, blast furnace
And black water, fire sloughing on the surface
Like a skin, the stars blowzy as moths . . .
Going west, I thought, was going in.
God had something to do with machinery,
One hard edge set against another,
Towns strict as church pews in the face of sin.
I thought it was a word, one half
Of the boxcars I watched rattling past.

Flashbulbs

Emsworth and evening, 1958—
The wedding reception of some
Cousin or other far shoal
Of the family blood. The bride
Is generic white veils of lace
Being spun about the room,
My aunts in attendance, uncles
Already drifting off to talk
About handicaps, the hapless
Steelers, and how things are
At work. Each in turn smiles
Back into the sudden tungsten
Of the flash, while in the sky
Over Pittsburgh stars burn
Like fiery ingots, the great
Rivers darken and rise into
The night. Playing on the side-
Walk, we feel them on our skin,
Smell the leaves of the ginkgo
Branching there above us
In the fusty summer air. But
This evening's real treasure
Already glimmers in our hands:
The small, frazzled bulbs
We've brought out here to dash
Against the pavement. Reveling
In the repeated claps of air
Into their vacuums, we scattered

The sidewalk with glass and
The pocks of small explosions,
Plosives which had rendered up
Their one emphatic sound—
That syllable of darkness
Spoken from inside the light.

Granville Beitel

Saturday evening: my cousin on the phone
    With Latin and the death of my uncle,
        The marrow of his bones
    Continuing to fail him on stairway

And landing, sheets he'll be washed from,
    The sleeves of his coats . . .
        His death makes me a boy again,
    Alone, riding the spark-charged streetcar

To the end of the line in Emsworth,
    Carrying my suitcase and Sunday clothes
        Down the cobblestones of Green-
    Wood Avenue, ablaze in my own bones.

One block away, the near lane
    Of the Ohio River Boulevard rushed
        Blankly into the Midwest.
    All around me, the incredible alleys

Showed me why houses faced the streets,
    Made me mad for climbing into trees,
        Cupboards, the dark coal cellars
    And foundations of the world.

Even now, twenty years later in the hills
    Above my house, I remember darkness
        Like a time of year, a temperature
    I could climb through, out of my bones,

Like leaving home for good. Beneath me
       The flat guttering flames of trees
              Flash upon their waters. The bleary
       Constellations wheel across the sky.

All night long I have been up here,
       Watching in the darkness of his death
              For that one faint star, burning
       Toward daybreak like a shuttling car.

IV

Entering the Oven

when the sun went down, and it was dark, behold a smoking furnace
—Genesis 15:17

Pittsburgh, 1965: the graveyard shift
At U.S. Steel.
            Most nights nothing
Is the hardest thing we have to do,
Look busy,
          or wake in time for lunch
At 4:00 A.M. Men I work with
Enter their talk
          like neighborhoods
Where wives wait all night long
To be filled with something
          other
Than sleep, where love is metal
And sex the violence
          of marriage.
They uncork themselves like thermoses,
Mouths filled
          with the crural air.
Pips they spit out fall into the yard—
Seeds
          that are trying to take hold,
Hours later, in the first dead wash
Of dawn.

*

There are ways to sleep
Which are learned, ways to take your-
Self up in your arms
                        and not unravel
Through whistle and dream,
Black night or nightmare
                              on the floor.
You tuck in you. Overhead,
Cranes shuttle,
                        carrying the fire.
And above the bombed-out landscape
Of the mills
                the moon slides
On its greased tracks down toward
This life,
              slivering across
The black water, the nothing glazing
The mirror's back:
                        glimpses
Sleep sends nightly through
The slow pull
                and entropy of the blood.

          *

It is the ear which anticipates
In darkness,

                        high noon
Out of the night, the dense
Flickering strobe
                        of the lightning.
The sky cracks open as above
Another country,
                        and Pittsburgh,
Our Toledo, flashes, heat climbing
Like catwalks
                        to the ceiling,
The smokestacks the sky climbs over,
Flaming into tongues.
                        All night
We watch dippers portion the air
Out almost completely,
                        the cast-
Blue light twitching in the dark.
Watch the world take shape,
                        inside
And out, in a great confluence
Of Augusts,
                        light crack
Out of thunder like The Light.

        *

On breaks,
                cigarettes are another fire
We fill with, faces rising like smoke

Into rafters
                and clerestory,
The crane tracks where my grandfather
Fell from 1907
                and shattered his back
On this floor. His pocketwatch holds
That moment,
                the guillotine of time.
There where balance was everything,
The mainspring snapped,
                        time was out,
All the things that carried him came
Streaming from his pockets
                        to fall
Like fists on my grandmother's door
When the first men stood
                        out there
In the cold, holding their caps,
And she saw gray
                in their faces,
The ashen light, how even the snow
As it fell
                was gray as mill smoke,
The way it would always be.

                *

In the darkened heart
                of this circle

We can almost see the garbage
Steaming in its pile,
                    the crane's
Huge, magnetic disk hovering above it.
Can almost hear,
                    before we hear
For real, the floor crawling
With rats,
                    their metallic claws,
Eyes bright as rivets.
Up from the river,
                    from the sewers,
They swarm, black as water beneath us,
Belly into the pile,
                    jaws seeping,
Eye-deep in hunger and their
Scavengers' ecstasy
                    of compounds
Breaking down. Are still ravening
When the juice is cut
                    and that disk
Slams like gravity into ground zero
On the mill floor.
                    Lights clang on.
The magnet lifts from its bull's-eye—:
Lottery
        of the night's random dead.

*

Night after night the man with
The white hat
                    and all the pens
Calls out names and accidents from
The preceding shifts,
                        chants up
Cuts and bruises, broken bones,
Lost fingers
                and how to hold on
To our own on the jobs he is sending
Us to.
        We gather up tools, the hands
Of our gloves, move to our labors
Among shale heaps and oil,
                            grime
And sheet metal—to the nine-runged
Ladders of hell
                    under furnaces,
Shoveling in flues, in tunnels
Where water seeps like rats,
                                lathes
Drop their spinnings—ovens
And coalbins
                in the great house
Of night, the bellies of machines
Which never sleep,

                    but sing
Through their gears like the heavens.

        *

Tonight, as usual,
                    evening's flared
Like a slag heap down the rim
Of the sky,
                    mills cast their sunsets
On the waters, and we are entering
The oven,
                    tearing a wall of fire-
Bricks out of number 4's 120° depths.
As long as we can bear it,
                              we hurl
Crowbars at a wall blank as the face
Of a whale,
                    rush back out for salt
And water, to put out our feet,
And sit clothed
                    by something other
Than flames. Cooled off, we reenter
That kingdom of heat
                          where the soles
Of our shoes start to smoulder,
Shirts flower with holes
                          like small,

Dark stars . . . until, finally, we are
Walking on fire
                    as if born to it,
Burning by our bodies, the candles
Of the spine.
                    Even outside
We can smell it, sitting exhausted
And smoking
                    in a last blue of heaven
The color of steel.

V

Since History Is a Marriage of Geography and Race

All week I've been thinking about
The house on Interboro Avenue
With its wood floors and throw rugs
And old upright piano, about

The amazing flights of laundry
Down the stories of its chute.
For the first time in years
I've remembered that bottle of holy

Water and sitting next to my aunt
At the crowded table, after
They'd buried my Uncle Arch.
I've been thinking about the landing

At the top of the stairs
In the old house on Sixteenth Avenue,
How I felt like I were floating
When standing there,

Up into a corner of the room.
I've even dreamt about those waters
In Emsworth lapping at the curbs,
About one cousin's heirlooms

And another's breasts, the round
Dark of the carbarn where trolleys
Were kept overnight. All week long
I've found myself surrounded

By basement shelves and closets,
The green fire of the sycamores
Whose branches shook my sleep.
I've been struck by the gnosis

These places bring to life.
By a friend's father who listed
His old home address no matter
Where he was living. Unlike

Me, he knew he'd return in time
To join the light which angled
Across the floorboards, the wood-
Grain gleaming in its patient lines.

The Origins of Evening

for my uncle, Arch Sharp

The telephone—
Every time it rings
Someone has died,
Someone has lain down
In the living room
Or sat up all evening
To surprise you
With the news
That you are alone,
That the body is simply
Another furniture
And filigree of dust
Or heaven is a house
Like in the movies,
Full of shrouded rooms.

*

All that afternoon
I look for my uncle
In piles of laundry,
The backs of drawers
Dark with vests and ashes.
Evening begins
In the burrs which cluster
To the laces of his shoes,
Dusk comes to a sky
Scuffed and bruised

As the hands I remember
Holding nothing
At last, except each other,
The hands
Of ink and tobacco.

*

Here, across more years
Than make any sense,
I study my own hands,
Seeing how they are
No longer mine alone.
Scarred and twisted
Into their time
Is everything I've held,
Everything I've had
To let go.
There are absences
I carry, like the end
Of day, handfuls of light,
There are winds still
Dying in the cupboards.

The Closet

This is the first dark
    I will not be lifted from,
 Out of my mother,
Though I would gladly be head down
    Again above her, thrashing
  Like a fish in the air.

This is the dark
    In which I turn fish for real,
 The side of my face
Pressed flat against the floor,
    Down where a knife's edge
  Worth of air is scaling.

It's a way of being dressed
    Which means staying home,
 Closer to my clothes
Than ever, feeling how they hang there
    In the dark, fabrics
  Quietly breathing.

Again and again I think
    Of how I might unlock the door
 By prayer or will
Or imagining myself back to before it shut
    Like the darkness
  All about me,

And I began to feel
        The way I do in church—
Mouth stuffed, bones
On fire on the dark barbs of horsehair,
                Thinking again of Moses
        Who was hauled from

        His waters, of breach-
                Birthed Jonah and the Jesus
    Who went to sea.
Of my own front yard where the maples
                Are burning light,
        Cellars and gardens,

        The undersides of rocks
                Where the world grows things
    Amazing as a boy in a closet,
Ears ringing with the sea, with the sound
                Of babies being lifted,
        Amniotic and blue,

    Into the limitless prospects of the breath.

Song for My Father

For whatever the reason, years ago,
    The woman my father married
        After my mother's death
    Lied that he was dying. That spring
I sat watching him go wrong
    In the blighted arms of the maple,
        Its leaves red as the crab.
    I dreamt of locusts swarming up
His throat, and was afraid to write
    This poem or answer the phone
        For I saw how dying closes down
    On ways the future might go.
Throughout the summer I thought of him
    Grown white and knotty
        As his ankles, the fear he'd out-
    Prescriptioned laid finally to rest,
There in Florida's alien soil. Old men
    Should be lean and bright
        As lizards, they should blink back
    At the indifferent sun in scale-eyed
Contempt since there is nothing
    They have failed to suffer
        While feeling their veins turn thin
    And dry as light. An old man
Is more than music and pride,
    Good meat or a worn bone.
        Even then I thought of how for one
    It would be like lying down on water,

The waves foaming upon a shore,
    Weed-strewn and streaming with
        The retreating tides, he'd never
    Have to struggle up once more.

Swimming Lessons

I have swum through libraries
—MELVILLE

This morning, for the first time
    In years, I share my nakedness
        With strangers, changing again
            In a locker room among familiar

Echoes and old men gathered for
    Their daily swim like poor, talc-
        Colored angels come to leave
            All human heaviness behind.

The summer I learned to swim
    They'd be there, toweling dry
        And talking, while we stripped
            And hurried on our suits to slip

Into that underworld of light
    Webbing over water, downstairs
        In the Homestead Library where
            Some luminary built the pool.

Closing my eyes, I breathe in
    The astringent scent of chlorine,
        Half expecting to open them again
            And find myself wading through

95

The same old sequence of strokes,
Or hanging from the kick rail
Where I tried my best to flutter
The way I'd been shown—

Wondering why I never turned
Weightless when even librarians
Floated, stories above us,
Among the dust and dreamy motes.

When the whistle finally blew,
My legs would settle below me
In a warp of watery optics,
And once again I'd haul myself

Up out of water into my nakedness
And weight, just as I'll do
This morning, to shower amid
Echoes and the glare of memory's

Recognitions, there and on the worn
Bench before my locker, the towels
Of the wet, replenished angels
Billowing about them like sails.

The Adorations

School nights were best.
We'd gather in the granular wilderness
Of dusk and wait, first
For the streetlights, and then
Our shadows, front and back,
On the sidewalks as we hurried,
Walking the blood back down
From our cheeks, our ears

Which seemed to be buried
Inside the uterine folds of shells.
Later, in backyards, from
The tarred roofs of garages,
Or standing stalk-still in gardens
Like a strange nocturnal crop,
We'd watch for lights to come on
In windows we knew by heart,

The first female shapes to appear
naked as the constellations.
Trembling in that darkness,
We'd watch women go through
The small, usual rituals
We thought no man had seen
From inside such rooms.
We thought our eyes alone

Had touched them as softly
As they touched themselves,

Or glowed about the bodies
They seemed unaware were vestal
And filled with the moon's
Round fires. They were holy
And never seemed to know it,
Would not have dreamt

They were worshipped so
By boys in their own backyards—
We who would have altered
Nothing about them, asking
Only that they go on nightly
Entering all the astounding
Dimensions of the flesh.
All year we huddled out there

In secret, hungering for visions,
Unwilling to miss a thing.
As they drifted toward sleep,
The ashes from our cigarettes
Would fall onto the ground and glow
Like tiny candles. Rapt
And votive as acolytes, we'd toe
Them out, slowly, one by one.

Letter to Russell Barron

Most likely whatever glimpse
We caught of each other
Will turn out to have been the last one.

I don't know where a solitary one
Of you are, or even if you are all alive.
As much as I might like to,

I don't believe I'll ever make it back
To sit in Chiodo's sipping beer
Just across the street from WAMO,

Or that the currents are going
To carry me home. Russell,
You're the one who turned me round

To rhythm-and-blues, 45s with labels
Luminescent as tropical plants.
I can't tell you all that they've meant.

Without them, I might never have reached
Muddy Waters, Illinois Jacquet,
Or those horses

Cantering along the keyboard
In Tatum's deft and stately hands.
If you made it over the river,

I hope you got farther than the suburbs.
That evening I was terrified by your father
Bulling his bulk into the furniture,

Drunk and wheezing like a narrow gauge,
There on the living room floor—
I hardly knew the first thing about singing.

Listen, Russell, wherever you are,
I hope that from time to time
You rise up in the heart of your house

In the soft mammal dark.
I hope you have a woman like I do
Who hasn't contracted terminal good taste.

I'm sorry about the ways we lose
One another along our drift of days,
That the trolleys have vanished

Along with the Mystery Train.
And I'm sorry about the Friday
I never showed up.

I was with that lovely armful
Of lonely bones, skinny Margie Stulginski,
And most likely I'd do so again.

Sitting in the Dark

But this is wonderful, three o'clock
    And the whole place empty!
        I look down the dark
            Varnished length of bar wood

On which there is nothing
    But colors floating just inside the depth.
        We used to call them *matinees*,
            These afternoons cleared from

Whatever dulled us. Sometimes
    We'd wind up on the Hill, at Crawford's,
        Where my father listened to Erroll Garner,
            And we heard good solid combos

Playing so hard the bruise-
    Colored bones glowed within their skins.
        No music is next best to the real thing.
        It's quiet in here.

Only when he brings me
    My second beer will Walter stand before me,
        Rocking on his heels, and ask
            If it's still raining, or how I feel

About the shrill, preppy Texan
    In the White House. Then
        He'll move back to stand motionless
            In that light like yellow paint,

Staring off into the 73 years
  His life has taken to get there.
    He does not know it but the way he feels
    Can be transfigured

Only through the coils
  Of certain trumpets, passages of air
    Across the sweet shimmed backs of reeds.
    I'd like to tell him what he has

Is called "Sitting in the Dark,"
  But am silent instead. What can I say, really,
    To this stoic little man,
      Except *yes* or *no, not much,*

Or *see you around?*
  What good would it do him, listening
    To names he doesn't come home to,
      Four to the bar?

Last Things

How fully they are no longer with you—
    The empty rooms, ties knotted for the last time,
        Records you played for years, then slipped
Back into their jackets and never heard again.

All your life things have fallen away
    Without you even knowing. You have gone
        Out to the car and left and never even looked
Up into the mirror where the world already

Was twice as far away. The light falling
    Like slag upon Homestead, the rind of light
        Above Carmel, were skies you thought to have
Forever. You thought you'd always have a place

To come back to, where you could stand again
    At the windows, watching the locust
        Blossom among its thorns, the banked fires
Of the roses. The last time you went back

People who'd moved in had ripped out everything:
    Shrubs and trees. That was the first time in years
        You followed the river to Emsworth,
Asking your uncle, "Do you know me?"

Now you have eaten the last meal at that table
    After washing your hands and folding them
        In prayer and having to swallow whatever
You'd been fed. You have loved one woman

For the last time. And now, tonight, you have
    The last dream in which you wear the shirt
        Of wrinkled water, that flowering cloth
Which begins to open, looming the vacant air.

Aubade

Early morning, the 18th of June,
I wake in the kind of heaven
Annibale Carracci hung on the ceiling
Of the Farnese Gallery.

The day flares like copper
From the leaves of the beech,
The wind chimes bright as apples
In the clear, burnished Italian air.

Perhaps it is only an old grammar
I am beginning, again, to hear,
The chance flurries of Vivaldi,
Their complexities of simple delight,

But somehow it does not seem strange
To find the 17th century
Flourishing here in Pennsylvania,
Early mornings, late in the spring.

All night I have been dreaming
Of the sadness of gloves, of skins
In which the body is missing,
Like trying to remember home.

Now I see once more
How the body comes back like the world
Waking through all five senses
And the ones beyond.

Every day my father woke to a glare
Like water breaking across his face,
Bathed in the cold dawn of Pittsburgh,
And walked away uphill. No music,

No squares of sunshine unhinging themselves
Like whole piazzas of heaven
From the ceilings of Rome. Only the trolley
Swaying beneath its grid of sky,

The pigeons in Pittsburgh,
Ringed and colored as oil slicks.
Down in the garden I watch the mockingbird
That sang by my window last night.

His breast soft and shadowed,
Wings half out, he hops down a row
Of bean poles, as if in love
With such intervals of distance and vine

And the way he moves among them,
The way this morning
Even my father walks with trumpets
Clear to the top of the hill.

Notes

"Fathers and Sons." The actual "Bedlam" referred to was the Dixmont State Hospital, a mental health facility, which has since been closed.

"Seeing Pittsburgh." The packet alluded to, a tourist brochure, was published by Minsky Bros. & Co., Pittsburgh, Pennsylvania. Some of the details in the poem are drawn from it, others imagined. Here, as elsewhere, "Pittsburgh" is meant to denote a region and milieu as well as the city proper.

"On First Viewing *The Deer Hunter*: Boyd Theater, Bethlehem, 1978." The film opens with a shot of the mills along route 837 in Clairton (its ostensible setting), one of the many industrial towns flanking the Monongahela River just south of Homestead, Pennsylvania.

"Rogation Sunday." The sermon mentioned at the poem's conclusion, from which the italicized words are taken, concerns the story of Lazarus as recounted in John 11.

"Letter to Russell Barron." WAMO are the call letters of what was at the time, in the 1950s and early 1960s, a great rhythm-and-blues station located in Homestead.

"Song for My Father." The poem takes its title from the classic Horace Silver composition by that name.

"Sitting in the Dark." The title is an allusion to a song, recorded for Bluebird in 1933 by Louis Armstrong and His Orchestra.